MY PLACE IN HISTORY

My Life on the TRAIL OF TEARS

By Max Caswell

Gareth Stevens PUBLISHING

Please visit our website, www.garethstevens.com. For a free color catalog of all our high-quality books, call toll free 1-800-542-2595 or fax 1-877-542-2596.

Library of Congress Cataloging-in-Publication Data

Names: Caswell, Max, author.
Title: My life on the Trail of Tears / Max Caswell.
Description: New York : Gareth Stevens Publishing, [2018] | Series: My place in history | Includes index.
Identifiers: LCCN 2017013561| ISBN 9781538203095 (pbk. book) | ISBN 9781538203101 (6 pack) | ISBN 9781538203118 (library bound book)
Subjects: LCSH: Trail of Tears, 1838-1839–Juvenile literature. | Cherokee Indians–Relocation–Juvenile literature. | Cherokee Indians–History–Juvenile literature.
Classification: LCC E99.C5 C227 2018 | DDC 975.004/97557–dc23
LC record available at https://lccn.loc.gov/2017013561

Published in 2018 by
Gareth Stevens Publishing
111 East 14th Street, Suite 349
New York, NY 10003

Designer: Bethany Perl
Editor: Joan Stoltman

Photo credits: Cover, p. 1 (Trail of Tears painting) courtesy of WOOLAROC MUSEUM, BARTLESVILLE, OKLAHOMA; cover, p. 1 (background) Natalia Sheinkin/Shutterstock.com; cover, pp. 1–24 (torn strip) barbaliss/Shutterstock.com; cover, pp. 1–24 (photo frame) Davor Ratkovic/Shutterstock.com; cover, pp. 1–24 (white paper) HABRDA/Shutterstock.com; cover, pp. 1–24 (parchment) M. Unal Ozmen/Shutterstock.com; cover, pp. 1–24 (textured edge) saki80/Shutterstock.com; pp. 1–24 (paper background) Kostenko Maxim/Shutterstock.com; pp. 5, 19 (map) Luchenko Yana/Shutterstock.com; p. 5 (Cherokee letters) JTGrafix/E+/Getty Images; p. 7 (newspaper) courtesy of the New York Public Library; p. 7 (John Ross) Wikipedia.org; p. 9 (Cherokee home) Marilyn Angel Wynn/Nativestock/Getty Images; p. 9 (bayonet) Anton Vasylenko/Shutterstock.com; p. 11 KennStilger47/Shutterstock.com; p. 13 (blackberries) Evelyn_Art/Shutterstock.com; p. 13 (mullein) Volodtmyr Nikitenko/Shutterstock.com; p. 15 Patricia Hofmeester/Shutterstock.com; p. 17 (Trail of Tears) Al Moldvay/Denver Post/Getty Images; p. 19 (three sisters) igorsm8/Shutterstock.com; p. 21 (chunkey stones) Nativestock.com/Marilyn Angel Wynn/Nativestock/Getty Images; p. 21 (Cherokee flag) Wikipedia.org.

Printed in the United States of America

CPSIA compliance information: Batch #CS17GS: For further information contact Gareth Stevens, New York, New York at 1-800-542-2595.

CONTENTS

Words in the glossary appear in **bold** type the first time they are used in the text.

They Want OUR LAND

February 10, 1838

I'm writing this to record the **plight** of my people, the Ani'-Yun' wiya'. We cleared the fields, prepared the soil, and fenced in fields. Now white people steal our livestock, burn our barns, and **loot** our homes.

A few years ago, gold was discovered near our home. Mother said white people would rush in to find the shiny rocks, and she was right. Her mother named me Awenasa, which means "my home." Soon enough, though, I fear I won't have a home.

Notes from History

The Cherokee, or Ani'–Yun' wiya', were the largest native group in the southern United States and are the only one in the United States with a written alphabet of their language. A 9-year-old Cherokee girl in 1838 might have been able to write in both English and Cherokee!

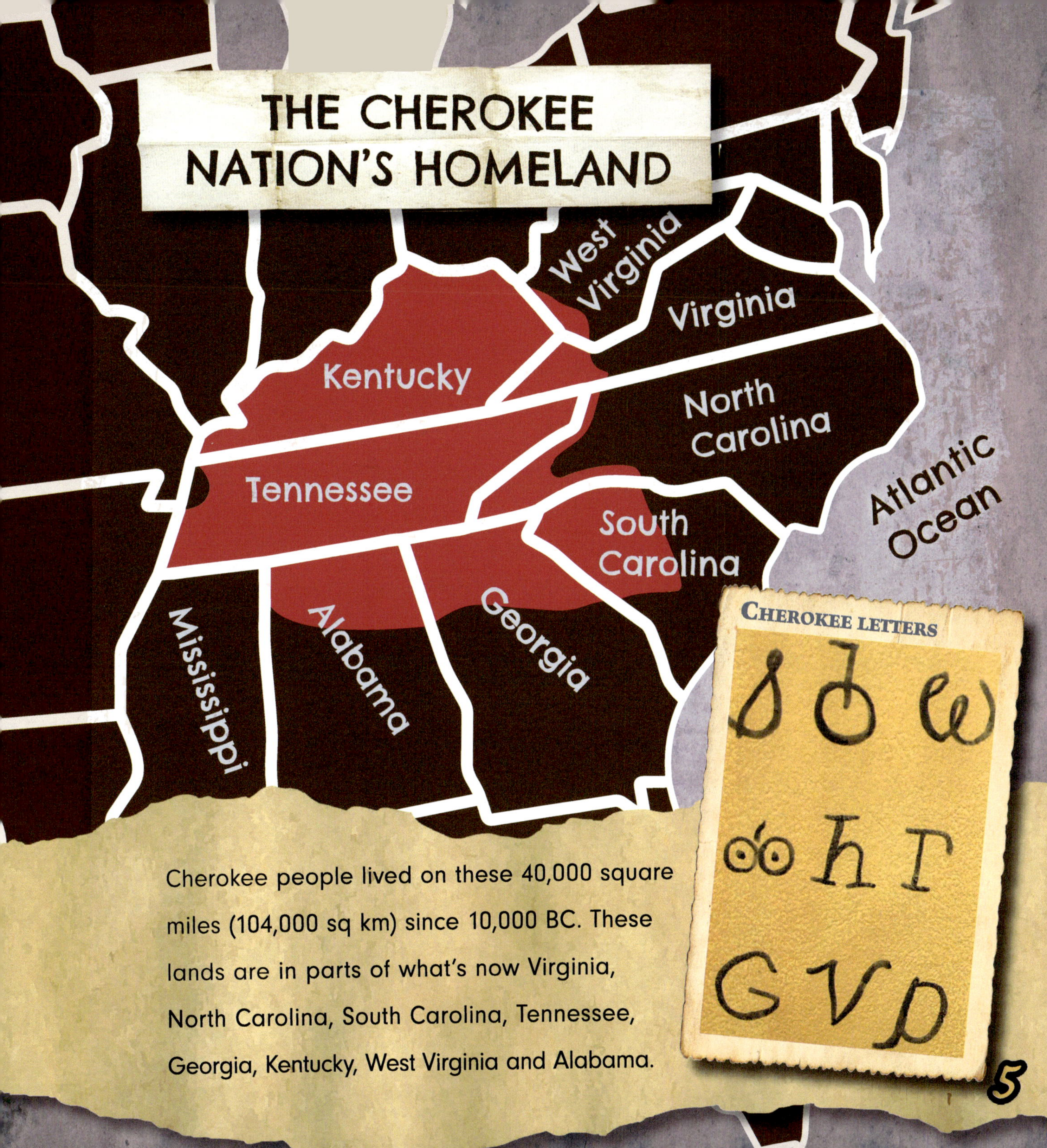

Cherokee people lived on these 40,000 square miles (104,000 sq km) since 10,000 BC. These lands are in parts of what's now Virginia, North Carolina, South Carolina, Tennessee, Georgia, Kentucky, West Virginia and Alabama.

Not Civilized ENOUGH

April 29, 1838

My people are much like white people. We speak and write in English. We dress like them. We have a government, a capital, and a **constitution**. We even have a newspaper. But they still don't see us.

President Andrew Jackson still holds up that false **treaty**, saying it gives the government our lands. The names of 16,000 Cherokee against the treaty were sent to the president right after the treaty was made law, but he won't listen.

Notes from History

A handful of Cherokee leaders signed the Treaty of New Echota in 1835, giving the Cherokee land to the United States in return for money, new land, and travel to the new land. They thought the treaty would keep their people alive.

ᏧᎴᎯᏌᏅᎯ.
PHŒNIX.

VOL. I. NEW ECHOTA, WEDNESDAY JUNE 4, 1828. NO. 15.

EDITED BY ELIAS BOUDINOTT
PRINTED WEEKLY BY
ISAAC H. HARRIS,

JOHN ROSS/TSAN-USDI

Tsan-Usdi, or John Ross, was a Cherokee chief who led for many years. He went to Washington, DC, many times in the years before the Trail of Tears to fight for his people's rights.

ROUNDED UP

June 12, 1838

My family and most Cherokee we know did as Tsan-Usdi told us to and remained on our land. Today, thousands of soldiers arrived to force us off our land. They went door to door, rounding up everyone. They pointed **bayonets** and gave us no chance to pack. They looted our homes as we headed toward our village's townhouse in chains.

At the townhouse, my mother sobs. She was a **council** member and met here many times for council business and events.

Notes from History

Hundreds of Cherokee escaped and hid in the hills of North Carolina during the roundups of 1838 and 1839. Today, their **descendants** make up the Eastern Band of the Cherokee Nation.

A CHEROKEE HOME

Troops were ordered to treat the Cherokee kindly. Instead, there are records that they dragged people from their home, often not even letting them put shoes on.

WAITING

August 24, 1838

They marched us west to Fort Armistead after they pulled us from our village. We've been sitting inside **stockades** day after day with little food and no clean water. Mother sneaks me any food she's given. I can see that Grandmother is weaker every day, so I pass the food to her. She's a medicine woman, so we all need her to be strong.

Illness has killed many. Sadness, Grandmother says, has killed many, too. She has no way to heal a broken spirit.

Notes from History

The Cherokee people headed west in 17 different groups formed at different forts, or strong buildings where soldiers lived, in Tennessee. Over 3,000 Cherokees were held at Fort Armistead for months in 1838. Many died.

STOCKADES

The law that moved the Cherokee and many other Native Americans off their land was called the Indian Removal Act. It was supposed to supply food, horses, oxen, and wagons for a journey west, but the soldiers stole much of the money and handled the rest poorly.

The March WEST

October 1, 1838

This morning just as the sun was rising, Tsan-Usdi led us in prayer. Then a horn sounded, and the wagons began to roll west. My little sister turned and waved good-bye to the mountains.

Grandmother managed to collect some blackberry root and mullein root from a meadow nearby before we set off. Her medicine is helping many swollen feet, knees, and hips tonight as I write. I haven't eaten much this week because I passed all my food on to her.

Notes from History

Only the sick, elderly, and young rode in wagons. Everyone else was forced to walk the entire journey, which was about 1,000 miles (1,600 km).

BLACKBERRY PLANT

MULLEIN

Cherokee medicine people asked a plant's permission before gathering it and left a small bead or other gift for the plant to thank it for its healing powers.

a sad JOURNEY

October 31, 1838

Like cattle, we are pushed to keep moving. Many began the journey crying, but now there's mostly silence. We put our heads down and drag our feet west.

We try to gather our food. So much has already been collected by groups that went before us. Grandmother taught us to only take every third plant to leave enough to grow. The groups before us were probably so **desperate** for food that they had to take everything they could find.

Notes from History

The first few groups of Cherokee in 1838 were led west by the US military. Many died. John Ross organized the later groups, making sure they were small enough they could feed everyone in the group by hunting and gathering food.

The Cherokee slept in wagons and on the cold, hard ground without a fire for warmth.

A Deadly WINTER

January 2, 1839

Heavy **sleet**, ice storms, snow, and terribly cold rain have made our journey harder since November. Our only **protection** from the bitter cold is our blankets, which we wear as cloaks by day.

Yesterday morning, Tsan-Usdi's wife gave her only blanket to my little sister, who's sick with coughing. Without a blanket, the poor woman's body turned to ice in the cold darkness, and she died. There's no time to **mourn** anymore. We bury her quickly by the trail and march on.

Notes from History

No one knows for sure how many Cherokee people died on the journey west. Guesses range from 4,000 to 8,000.

Some say 12 people were buried each night of that horrible winter. People died from **exhaustion**, lack of food and water, cold, and many kinds of illnesses.

ARRIVED

March 24, 1839

We've finally arrived on our new land. The land is bare, so we'll have to begin work right away. We must build homes and farms and prepare the earth for the three sisters. Hopefully, we have enough healthy people left to do the great amount of work that now needs to be done.

Some of our people settled here about 10 years ago, and they aren't happy we've arrived. We bring many more mouths to feed, and there's much anger between our leaders.

Notes from History

The trip usually took about 6 months. Because it was so painful a memory to talk about, few stories of the actual journey were passed down.

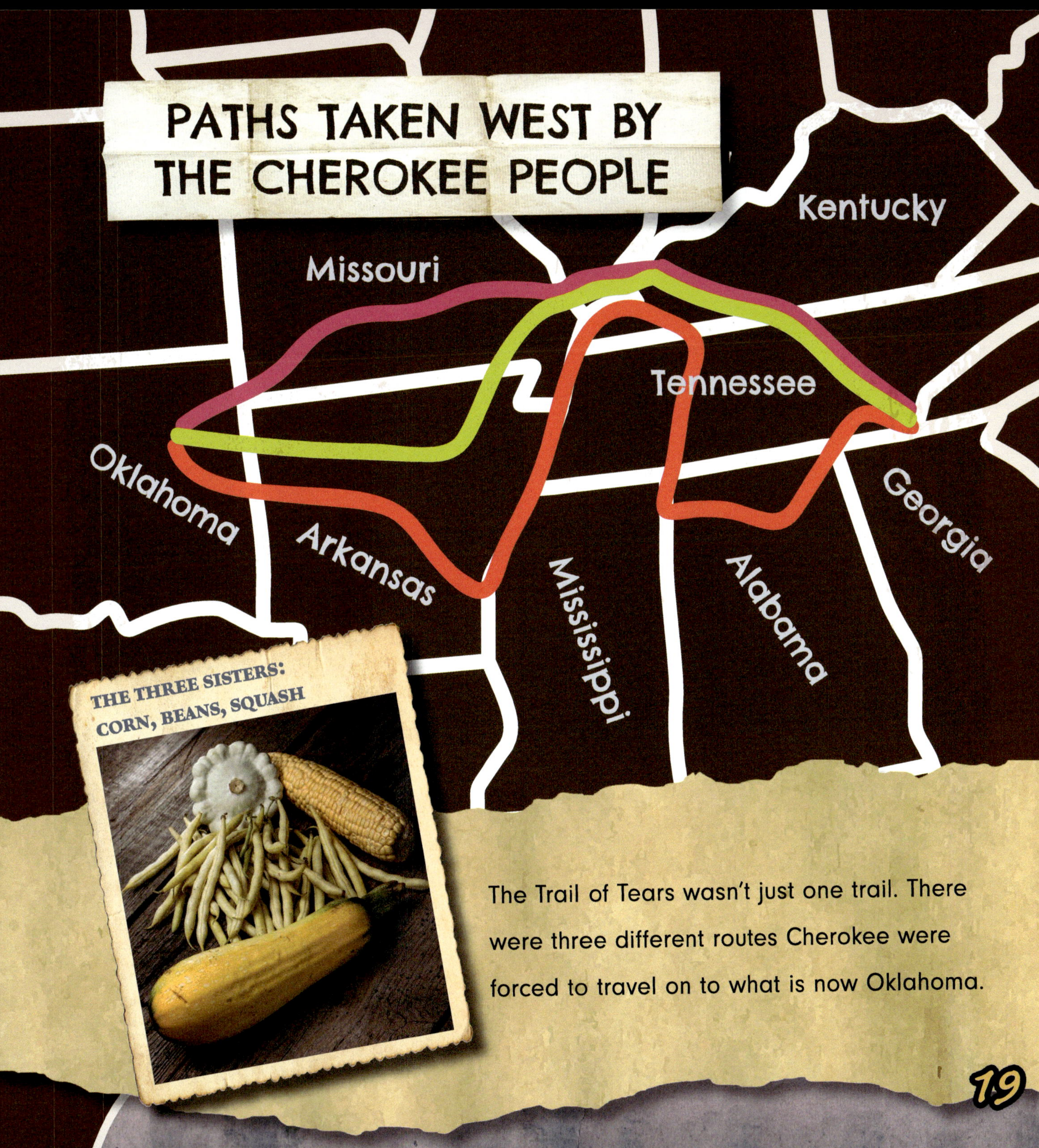

The Trail of Tears wasn't just one trail. There were three different routes Cherokee were forced to travel on to what is now Oklahoma.

I Hope We'll Be HAPPY SOON

June 20, 1839

Major Ridge and the other men who signed our land away were killed. Father said they were punished justly under Cherokee law for acting against our land and our people. I just wish the dying would stop so we can settle into this new life.

Our village's chunkey stone and poles were left behind. One of my favorite things to do in summer is watch a game of chunkey, so I hope they'll make a new stone and poles soon!

Notes from History

Played by many southeastern native peoples, chunkey is a two-person sport played with a smooth stone disk. The stone was hard to make and belonged to the village.

By September of 1839, the Cherokee people had a new capital, government, flag, and constitution. For many years, Tsan-Usdi continued to serve the 18,000 Cherokee people who walked west.

GLOSSARY

bayonet: a long knife that is attached to the end of a rifle and used for fighting in a battle

constitution: the basic laws by which a country or state is governed

council: a group of people who are chosen to make rules, laws, or decisions about something

descendant: a person who comes after another in a family

desperate: very sad and upset because of having little or no hope

exhaustion: the state of being extremely tired

loot: to steal things from a place during a war or after ruin has been caused

mourn: to feel or show great sadness because someone has died

plight: a very bad or difficult situation

protection: something that keeps a person or thing from being harmed or lost

sleet: rain that has been completely or partly turned to ice

stockade: a line of tall posts set in the ground around a place as a way to keep it safe

treaty: an agreement between countries or groups

For more INFORMATION

Books

Byers, Ann. *Life as a Native American on the Trail of Tears.* New York, NY: Cavendish Square Publishing, 2016.

Schwartz, Heather E. *Forced Removal: Causes and Effects of the Trail of Tears.* North Mankato, MN: Capstone Press, 2015.

Zardes, Cassandra. *Cherokee.* New York, NY: PowerKids Press, 2016.

Websites

Chunkey

cherokee.org/About-The-Nation/Culture/General/Chunkey

Read this description of the game of chunkey.

Indian Country Diaries: Interactive Map

pbs.org/indiancountry/history/interactive_map.html

This interactive map presents many moments in Native American history.

INDEX